wildiaries

First published 2024 by Wildiaries

Melbourne, Australia.

ISBN 9780645453591 Hardback

© Simon Mustoe, 2024

Illustrations, images, design and layout © Simon Mustoe, 2024

PINDITO

— SIMON MUSTOE —

wildiaries

WELCOME

In 1990 against what seemed impossible odds, Edi Frommenwiler persuaded the Indonesian government for a business permit to build PINDITO (PINisi-DIving-TOurism). For the following twelve years it was the only dive boat operating in eastern Indonesia.

In April 2022 Pindito celebrated its 30th year in operation. In this time they have created a rapport with locals throughout the remotest parts of Indonesia's Raja Ampat, Banda Sea and beyond.

It wasn't always this way though. In the Ayu Islands north of Raja Ampat in 1993 villagers appeared with spears and machetes. Edi's Indonesian wife Ella established a dialogue learning that rogue fishing boats had been destroying their reefs with cyanide. Reef preservation is essential for households whose income can be as little as a few dollars a month. Islanders depend on the ocean.

Conservation has always been a priority. Raja Ampat's national park boundaries were drawn up after Indonesian officials boarded Pindito and asked Edi to help draw the most important places on a map.

Those who stay on Pindito realise it isn't just a ship, it's also a family and home for two dozen crew and a place where guests are warmly received. As for entertainment, eastern Indonesia provides an endless supply of life-changing experiences.

Welcome and thank you for joining Pindito and continuing to make our journeys possible.

Simon Mustoe
Pindito expedition leader and ecologist.

Cover image: Pindito cruising in Raja Ampat near the head of the Dampier Strait. The island of Waigeo is in the distant background.

EDI & ELLA

Edi Frommenwiler was a mechanic, long-distance lorry driver, then adventure tour guide for ten years before he decided to embark on the journey of his life.

He worked for a European travel company and would get sent overseas to reconnaissance remote destinations. It was on one of these trips he met Ella who was working in a hotel in Surabaya, Indonesia.

Soon after falling in love, Ella and Edi travelled to Borneo and they built their life around a dream to construct a 38m long tourist ship ... they just happened to choose one of the world's most remote places in the world to do it.

Edi and Ella's greatest adventure though has been over 30 years of marriage raising two children, Ega and Thea. The relationship is still going strong, though Ella rarely comes out on the vessel these days and Edi has started to spend more time onshore with Ella (well, when he's not playing golf).

Meanwhile, Edi and Ella have proudly handed more of the management of Pindito to their son Ega who is pictured ringing the ship's bell on page 27.

1 9 9 1   2 0 2 2

PINDITO specifications

- Beam: 29 ft
- Length: 124 ft
- Speed: 7–8 knots cruising
- Economy: 5,000 litres per trip (~312 litres per guest)

THE MAKING OF PINDITO

Before crowd-sourcing became the rage, Edi garnered support from friends and families to fund the ship's construction.

It was 1991 on the island of Pulau Laut off Kalimantan when Edi, Ella and a team that included Edi's brother Peter and Ella's brother Toto, dug a dry dock and on 31 March laid the first timber keel of the Pindito.

Despite having no previous expertise in ship-building, Edi taught himself AutoCAD design. He designed the ship he wanted, one that would float for a hundred years and could be insured by German Lloyds.

Built from the strongest Indonesian timber, Pindito is almost over-engineered. The keel is made from a single piece of hardwood. Tens of thousands of bolts and a team of almost a hundred carpenters toiled to bring the ship to life before its launch in 1992.

Edi embraced local expertise but added new knowledge of metric measurements, tools and techniques. The ship yard still operates today.

PINDITO
2022
30 years anniversary

Pindito's size is most evident when viewed from inside the hull. It is wider than traditional Pinisi vessels. This allows the creation of eight sizeable cabins. It also makes the ship more stable and seaworthy.

BEHIND THE SCENES

Kitchen Crew

All successful ships run on the quality of their food. In Pindito's case this is a delectable fusion of authentic Indonesian and European-style dishes.

The kitchen staff are led by Edi's sister in law Febby (top right). They prepare four meals a day for all 16 guests plus the ship's 23 crew, starting with 'small breakfast'.

The kitchen is hidden away below the camera room with food handed to the ship stewards via a small service hatch. Which means the kitchen staff are often among the last people our guests get to know. This seems a bit unfair, given their importance – though guests are welcome to pop down and say hi at any time and they are the first to be introduced before the Captain's dinner at the end of the cruise.

It's our wonderful stewards that guests meet first. Always on hand to attend to everyone's needs, they service your rooms daily, make sure you have dry swimming towels, take breakfast orders and serve everyone in the mess hall.

Nitdyan (right) and Bukan (left) pass meals through the service hatch to our stewards.

Stewards Miko (right) and Nanang (left). Miko is Edi's nephew and is married to Nanang's sister. The mixture of relatives and lifelong friends adds to the family atmosphere.

The Wheelhouse Officers

Pindito has an open bridge policy and the Captain and officers are always present with a smile and 'selamat pagi' every morning. It's important to have someone on watch at all times. This includes when the vessel is anchored as stray currents can cause us to drag an anchor. Overnight and while steaming, the officers maintain watch for other ships, ensuring we can all sleep peacefully.

Toni on the wheel. The extended upper deck outside the wheelhouse window is the perfect place for guests to hang out, enjoy a drink, chat and watch the sun set over the ocean and islands.

Captain Casworo used to be a cargo ship captain before he joined Pindito in 2016. He has unsurpassed knowledge of the reefs throughout eastern Indonesia. This is no mean feat when you consider there are no maps to alert ships to the dangers of pinnacles and bommies hidden beneath the sea. After all, it's Casworo's job to get us as close as possible to any of the several thousand reef-fringed islands of eastern Indonesia. Together with the two officers, Casworo ensures we stay safe throughout every trip.

Crew Quarters

Having three crew for each of the key operational positions, including engineering and deck hands, means two crew are always on shift at any time.

This keeps everyone nicely rested while ensuring there is always someone watching out for problems before they arise (one of the reasons Pindito is such a safe ship).

Officer Mugi. Every crew member is earning hours towards their marine qualifications and may one day captain their own ship.

Engine Room

A ship can't go anywhere without its engine. The engine room is a cramped and hot space that has to be monitored regularly. Pindito has a Yanmar 6HA2M-WHT PS 350 horsepower engine. It also has two 40kW generators and a 2,000 gallon fuel tank, capable of doing 1,300 nautical miles. Fresh water is created using a reverse-osmosis desalinator supplying more than enough for the crew and guests each day. And of course, there are four Zodiacs, each of which has an outboard motor. Then there are toilets, air-conditioners, a coffee machine and innumerable other devices. The workshop is stocked with spare parts and equipment to fix almost anything. An engineer's job is never done.

YANMAR

Rudy doing a routine engine inspection.

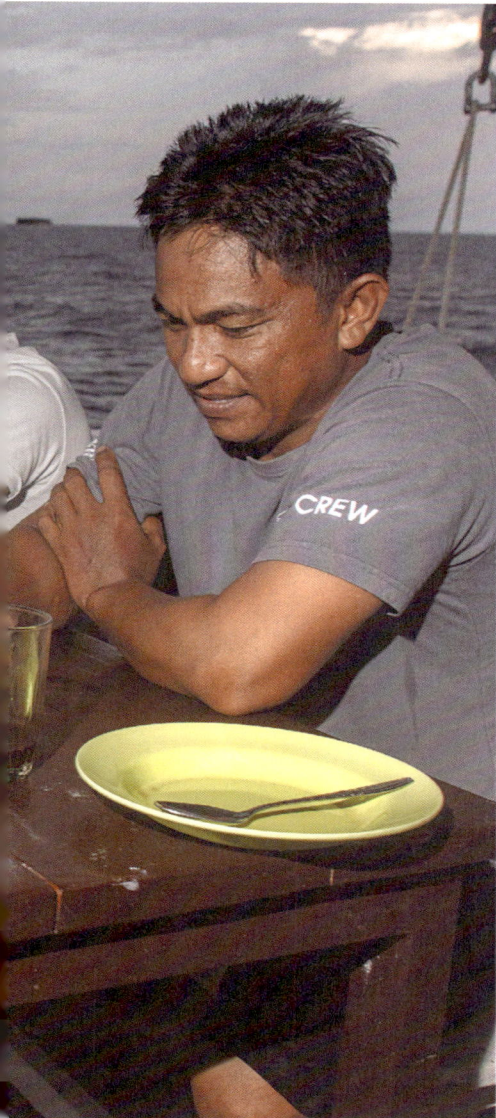

The Back Deck

Pindito recently acquired a fourth zodiac and positioned these off the side of the ship. This created a new space at the stern which the crew use for socialising and meal breaks. At other times you might find them congregating to look for whales on the very top deck above the bridge.

All in all Pindito has about 23 crew. With eight-hour rotations of duty this means there are two crew for every key position at any moment.

Among the few times you witness the full working contingent is when you are returning from a swim. The crew line up to welcome guests on board with a cheerful 'helloooo'. They then get to work tending the speedboats, washing and hanging up wetsuits, rinsing cameras and refilling dive tanks.

Ega Frommenwiler rings the cowbell.

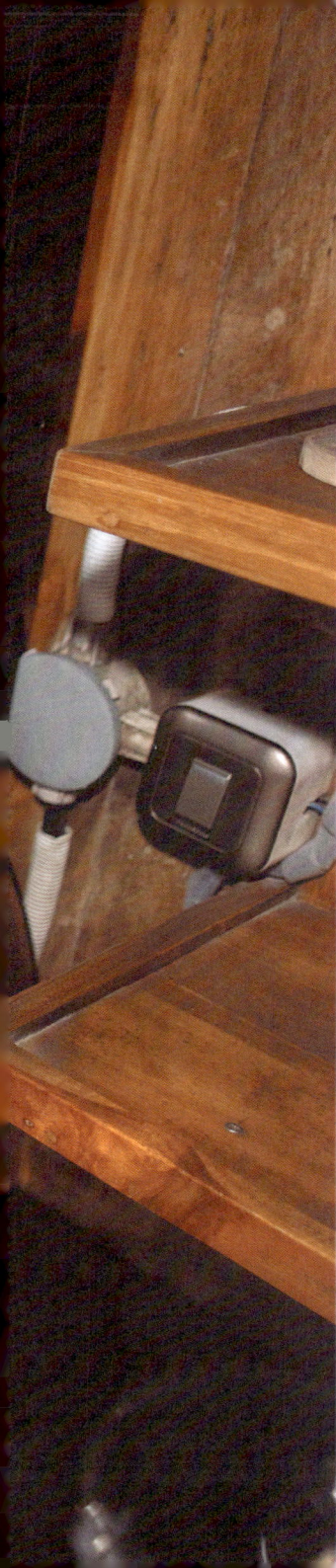

LET'S GET WET!

What's more fitting for a Swiss-Indonesian vessel than hanging a cowbell in a pinisi?!

Several times a day you'll hear two bells which means it's 15 minutes to go until snorkelling/diving. This is the time to gather behind the forecastle, suit up and prepare for your safety briefing – shortly after you'll likely hear Ape's signature call 'let's get wet' as we board our zodiacs.

Pindito's antique cow bell was gifted to the vessel by its investors in 1992 just after the ship launched. They carried it by hand from Switzerland and were ringing it as they walked through the airport in Bali. Edi couldn't believe his ears! Decorative bells like this have been handcrafted in Switzerland for centuries and the leather strap was custom made. Traditionally they were hung around the necks of cattle so herders could locate them grazing many miles away. On Pindito, it helps us find you, and you find your way to the deck at important moments.

If you're in the camera room, prepare to cover your ears. It's very loud!

Snorkelers photograph a Sargassum Frogfish. This was found by one of our speedboat drivers during a land visit while guests were enjoying cocktails on the beach!

The In-Water Team

Pindito has four in-water dive masters to look after up to sixteen guests, whether snorkelling or diving.

As well as ensuring your safety in the water, they have super keen vision, able to find the minutest and most camouflaged animals.

The dive team wouldn't be complete, however, without our speed boat drivers. As well as getting you to and from the swim site, they help lift heavy tanks and look after your gear.

Once you're in the water they stay nearby to offer a helping hand, always for rare emergencies but more often as a water taxi back upstream for snorkellers.

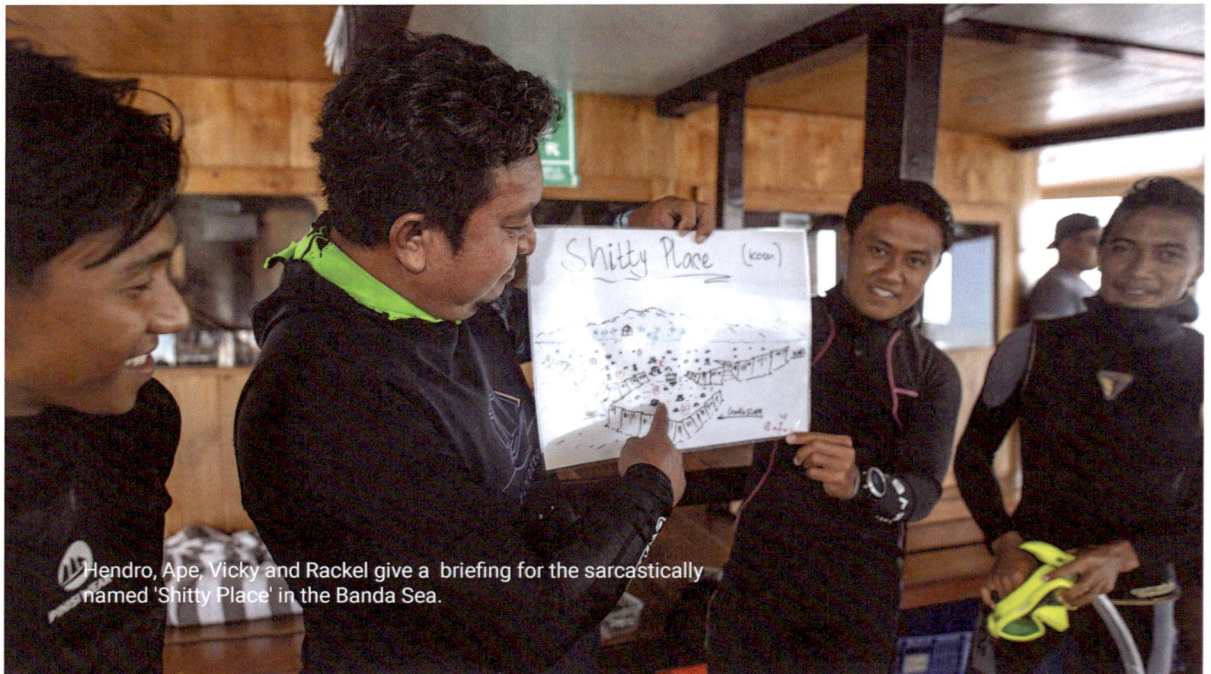

Hendro, Ape, Vicky and Rackel give a briefing for the sarcastically named 'Shitty Place' in the Banda Sea.

Speedboat driver Adrian has been with Pindito for a few years.

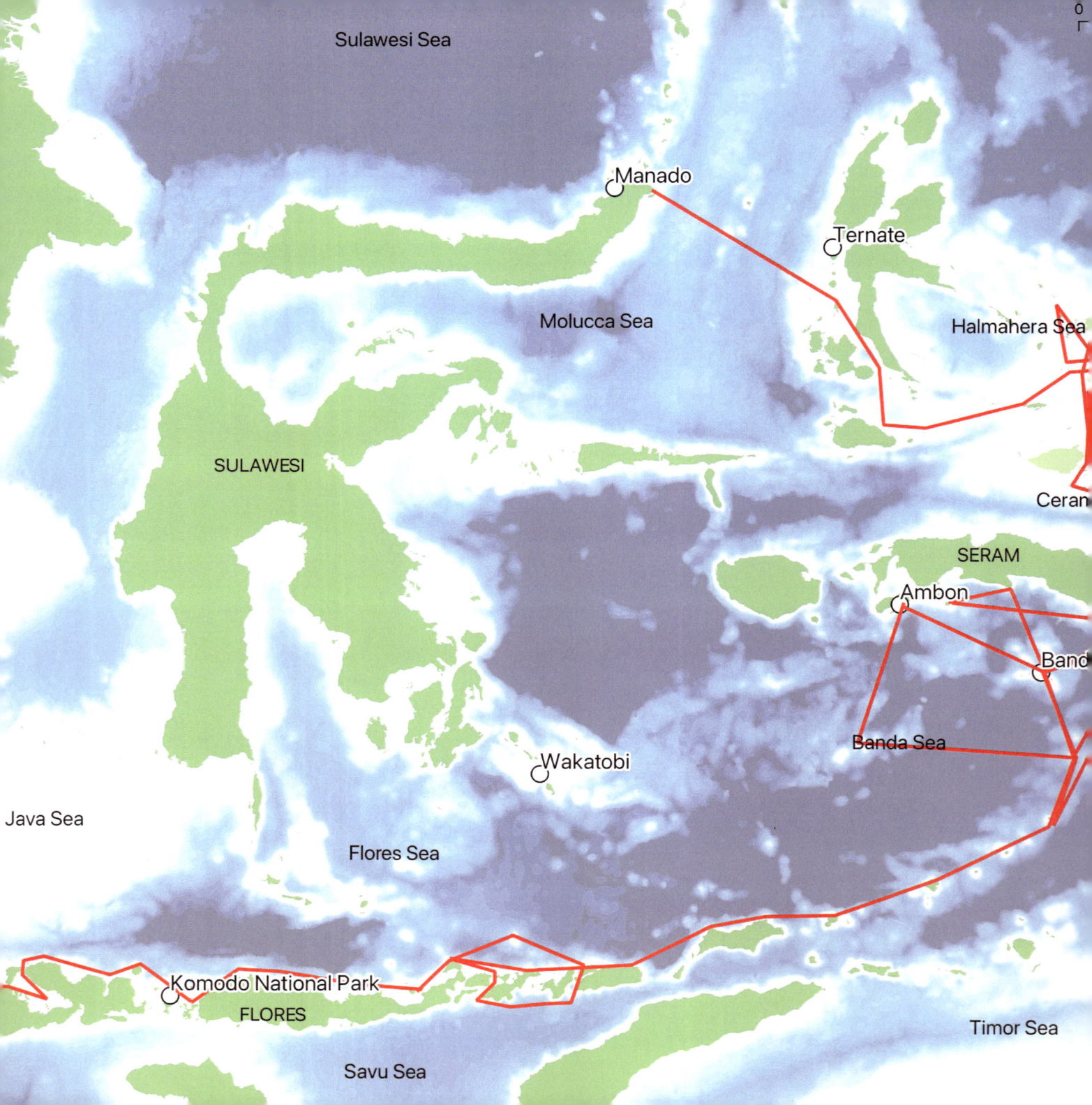

Sorong (Raja Ampat)

WEST PAPUA

Kaimana

ira

Arafura Sea

700 km

WHERE WE GO

Pindito cruises mostly run from about June to August in the southwest around Komodo and north of Alor. At this time of the year there are strong southeast trade winds and the seas here are more protected.

From about September to November we relocate to the Banda Sea as this is the only reliable doldrums period (when winds tend to be low). Then as the northwest monsoon begins, we head further east through December to March, to spend time in Raja Ampat and up north.

We often schedule longer trips between the two regions during the shoulder season, especially April / May. We also do occasional special trips into the Arafura Sea and Wakatobi.

Diving a pinnacle in the Banda Sea.

WHALE WATCHING

'When I started in 1992, I saw dolphins in the area but had no idea there were big whales around in Indonesian waters', says Edi.

'When I encountered the first whales, for me, it was a real 'wow' experience. A very exciting time'.

'Nowadays we know we have Orcas and even Blue Whales in the area', says Edi, 'I have seen Orcas a dozen times in the Banda Sea and Raja Ampat. The reaction of the guests is like, Blue Whales, Orcas .. this is something very special! Even Sperm Whales … there is something on every trip.'

Seeing unusual whales is very popular with guests.

'The other boats ask, what were you doing?' says our cruise director Ape (pictured far right).

We meander about after lunch looking for whales where we expect we might find them. Experts even join us on board for some trips. You can only dive or snorkel for about four hours each day, so we reckon, why not spend the rest of the time searching for whales and dolphins?

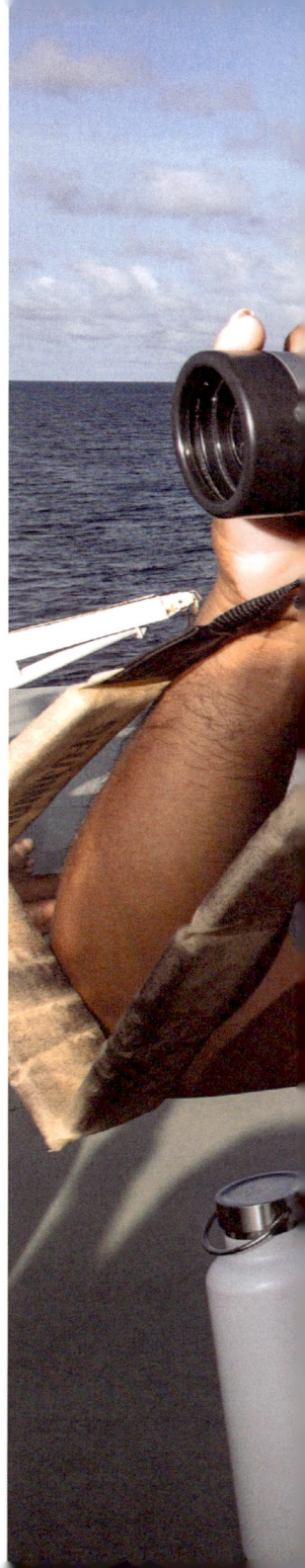

There are between 80 and 90 species of whale and dolphin in the world. Indonesian waters have about a third of these and a quarter can be seen in as little as one 12-day trip on the Pindito: Pan-tropical Spotted Dolphins, Spinner Dolphins, Fraser's Dolphins, Sperm Whale, Blue Whale, Killer Whale, Melon-headed Whale, False Killer Whale and Cuvier's Beaked Whales, to name a few.

Seeing whales has become part of Pindito's reputation. When the conditions are right, the crew will assemble at the very top of the vessel. At that height you can see ten miles in all directions.

As an extra incentive to find whales, we feed the Komodo Dragon in the wheel house (image, right). The reward is gifted to crew members when whales are sighted ... 'the dragon seems to be hungry', Dani will say. The effort can prove quite lucrative.

Killer Whales or 'Orca' (left) are occasional visitors. More commonly we see Short-finned Pilot Whales (centre). Guests enjoying watching dolphins riding Pindito's bow (right). Oceanic Bottlenose Dolphins on the bow of Pindito (next page).

INTO THE HEART OF THE CORAL TRIANGLE

There is nowhere on Earth that comes close to the Coral Triangle for diversity and abundance of ocean wildlife. Pretty much all of the world's coral life began in this area, which encompasses eastern Indonesia, the Philippines, Timor-Leste, parts of New Guinea and the Solomon Islands. Perhaps the most famous of all is Raja Ampat, located at its heart.

The entire Pacific Ocean empties through the islands of Raja Ampat, Halmahera and Sulawesi, rounding the Banda Sea where it cools by up to three degrees celsius before emptying into the Indian Ocean. This affects climate and food production as far as Africa and Australia. The Banda Sea is like an inverted himalayas, as deep as Mount Everest is high. It attracts the largest animal that ever lived on Earth, the Blue Whale, and European empires were built on its spices.

There is nowhere on Earth so profoundly diverse. This is Pindito's playground.

View from the lookout over Pienamo Lagoon in Raja Ampat.

Raja Ampat

Raja Ampat comprises a dizzying 1,800 islands surrounded by abundant coral reef.

Raja Ampat means Four Kings, after its four main islands: Misool, Salawati, Batanta and Waigeo.

The deep passage between Batanta and Waigeo attracts whales and dolphins. The narrow Saguin strait separating Salawati from Batanta marks the divide between four continental land masses. This further contributes to the region's diverse geology and wildlife.

In an area one-tenth the size of the Great Barrier Reef three-quarters of all the world's hard coral species exist. For 25 million years hardly a soul lived here. Species diversity rivals anywhere else on Earth.

A kaleidoscope of fish life over the extensive coral at Melissa's Garden.

Every crevice of calcium-carbonate rock is jam-packed full of wildlife, from the deepest coral to the top of forest-clad limestone mountains. For that is what the mountains are: ancient coral reef, lifted up on continental plates millions of years ago.

On the sheer coral walls hidden beneath these fortresses for biodiversity, pygmy seahorses live on gorgonian fans. Millions of mantid shrimps punch at passing plankton and oceanic manta rays cruise by.

Then there are the towering middens, prehistoric firepits and unmarked graves to be found in caves in Misool, evidence of a way of life forged by people here, long before Europeans came.

A Peacock Mantis Shrimp (left) uses its appendages to punch prey, They do this with the speed of a bullet, creating cavitation and immense heat. The shock is enough to stun or even kill its prey.

Rock art in Misool (top, right) has been dated to about 3,000 years. Some may be older. The skulls and bones (bottom, right) are thought to be Indonesian fishers. In the cave systems there are signs of prehistoric settlements but no-one really knows anything about the origin and history of these early settlers.

The limestone cliffs around Wayag and Misool are harsh environments with little soil or water. Orchids (left and centre) are well suited to these environments, using below-ground tubers to store nutrients and water. Pitcher plants go a step further. They supplement their nutrient intake by trapping insects in modified leaves shaped like a vase and digest them for food.

Banda Sea

The Banda Sea is epic; a place of myths and legends, pirates and sea monsters. It was the centre of a bloody spice trade for thousands of years. Oceanic processes drive climate worldwide, with sweeping currents emanating from depths that challenge the height of Everest.

From the bottom of the Weber Deep to the summit of Mount Binaiya, the highest peak on the island of Seram, is an elevation of over 10,000m.

A blue whale performs a deep dive. Here they spend an average of 2.5 minutes at the surface filling 1,500 litre lungs with air to restore oxygen to their body tissues. They then dive to 300m and lunge many times through the copepod layer (a type of plankton) before returning to the surface about 9 minutes later. They do this 24/7 for months at a time, during the most extreme periods of oceanic upwelling, driven by southeast trade winds.

Being in the Banda Sea gives one a sense of scale like nowhere else.

Hammerhead Sharks oxygenate their gills over submerged reefs, returning to hunt in complete darkness in the abyss. Seasonally, the largest animal that ever lived on Earth – the mighty Blue Whale – migrates from southern Australia to feast over monsoonal upwellings.

Hundreds of whales dive out of sight to penetrate the cold thermoclines, gulping thousands of gallons of plankton-rich soupy water. They redeliver nutrients to the surface, breathing life into the entire food chain, nourishing tuna, seabirds and helping support the livelihoods of tens of thousands of local fishers.

The village of Haya half way along the southern coast of Seram. The summit of Mount Binaiya can be seen in the background.

Fort Belgica represents a dark and bloody history. Today it attracts tourists and offers views of the surrounding landscape and a chance to remember the island's history.

The Twice Forgotten Islands

Banda Neira is an extraordinary place with a rich history. It it was the centre of the spice trade for thousands of years.

Archaeologists may have found recent evidence of villages from long before Dutch rule, where Bahasa Tana (language of the Earth) may have been spoken. It is a sacred language only sung in rituals. Sadly this ancient culture was all but lost at the hands of the Dutch East India company.

The Maulana Hotel heralds from a more prosperous time before the civil war. It was constructed by Des Alwi 'the uncrowned King of Banda' and is reputed to have hosted royalty and celebrities in the 1990s. It is being restored by Des Alwi's granddaughter Mita.

A Lesser Frigatebird hangs in the wind next to Pindito. The large wings make them uniquely adapted to gliding over the ocean. The knife-like beak is used to pluck food from the sea or, more commonly, harass other birds and steal food from them.

After the collapse of the spice trade was the first time the Banda islands were forgotten. The second was following a three year civil war in Indonesia in the late 1990s. The province was virtually cut off for many years and the islands economy is only just beginning to recover.

To the south are a chain of volcanoes including Manuk Island, which is probably one of the most important seabird colonies in the world. Tens of thousands of Lesser Frigatebirds, Brown and Red-footed Boobies nest among the searingly hot basalt rocks and steaming sulphur vents.

Locals travel hundreds of miles to fish below volcanic peaks, while droves of sea snakes hunt around thousand year-old barrel sponges below.

Seemingly endless highways of millions of fusiliers are one of the features of the Banda Sea.

Komodo

If you had to compare Komodo to anywhere it might be the fertile plains of Africa. You get the feeling animals are roaming everywhere. It's a more dynamic environment than Raja Ampat; a younger landscape shaped by volcanoes with a mixture of white and black sand reefs, iron-red sea cliffs and dry forested hillsides.

In a less wildlife-rich location, this fertility would be a disaster, leading to stagnation. Instead, in Komodo, every scrap of nutrient that pours off hillsides is quickly consumed by creatures in the sand.

Between volcanic boulders is a difficult place for coral to hang on so it falls to other animals to reap the rewards and keep the system in balance.

There is so much life that animals even live on other animals (and sometimes on the animals that live on animals). The Coleman Shrimps ride on the backs of Fire Urchins for example. There are octopus, frogfish, seahorses and a huge variety of nudibranchs to be found.

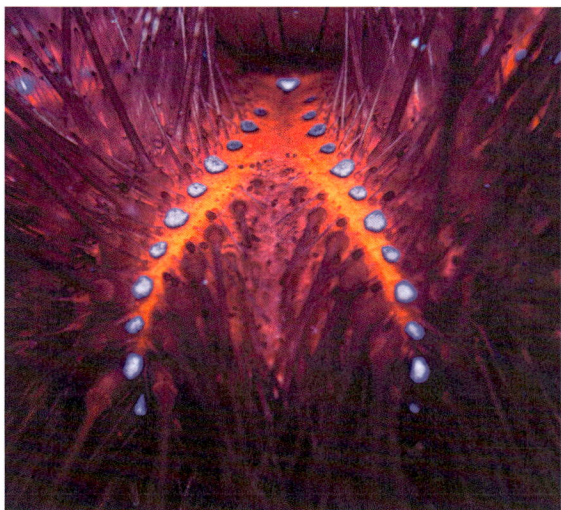

A colourful reef at Sanguang. It's very different to the hard coral reefs people are used to seeing but a hundred times more animals are to be found living among it.

Komodo also has a mixture of more traditional
looking coral reef which supports an unusually
rich mixture of fish life.

Elsewhere, strong currents smooth the seafloor. For example, Manta Rays and Unicornfish cruise over the moonscape of Karang Makasar.

Here, there are wide open plains of coral rubble, exposed by crystal clear cool water from the south. A diverse infauna lives among the rocks but have to keep their heads down, as they exposed to brutal currents several times a day.

Divers and snorkelers can experience this on casual drift dives here, or in an exhilerating ride through the aptly named 'shotgun', where swimmers are sucked over or through canyons between islands, emerging in the calm waters either side.

A whale shark in Saleh Bay. Most of the sharks here are males and range from about 5-8m long. During the day they descend to feed on lantern fish and plankton.

Pindito usually cruises to Komodo stopping at Saleh Bay where hundreds of Whale Sharks congregate. Here, the ominous outline of Mount Tambora dominates the skyline to the east – site of the largest eruption in human history. Local bagan fishing boats cast nets and light at night, attracting fish, plankton and sharks.

The locals save a bit of food for the whale sharks and offer a chance for guests to swim alongside these gentle giants as they guzzle plankton poured into their mouths from the surface.

Dragons of Komodo

Of course the region is synonymous with one its most famous residents, the Komodo Dragon. A trip to see these giant cousins of lizards is a must for anyone visiting the area.

Early morning on Rinca usually provides the best conditions. As the sun rises the dragons begin to warm up and start moving.

Don't let their slow demeanour trick you. They are pounce predators waiting for an unsuspecting victim to come near enough to strike. So, it's best to maintain a safe distance.

Tales of their toxic saliva are probably over-emphasised. Recent research shows they are simply formidable predators. Their teeth do most the work.

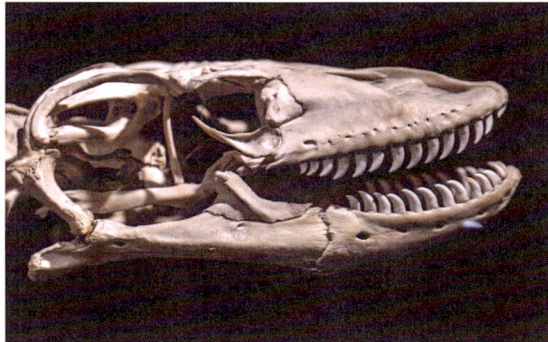

Grand Blue

Edi Frommenwiler has been documenting ocean wildlife on film between Raja Ampat and Bali since 1993. In that time he has done 14,000 dives and the equivalent of nearly 600 full days underwater!

This archive of Coral Triangle wildlife is irreplacebable. It's the biggest single resource on Earth, comprising over 16,000 film clips of more than 1,000 species of wildlife.

Incidentally, this is why Pindito is so well set up for photographers and film-makers.

Edi's efforts have culminated in the product of Grand Blue, a project to put all his shots online. The aim is to have it become an educational resource to help inspire a new generation of ocean conservationists.

The archive can be supported by visiting the website and signing up here:

https://grandblueproject.com/

GRAND BLUE PROJECT

Edi diving with his 'baby'. Photo by Reidar Opem.

The Pindito Band

Throughout your trip you might hear music emanating from the back of the ship.

Many of Pindito's crew come from Ambon, which has a long tradition of Indonesian folk music. At the end of each cruise and after the Captain's dinner, the whole ship's crew emerge to sing the guests some favourite songs.

Nusaniwe (right) is a popular Ambonese folk song that has been covered in almost every musical style imagineable and performed by some of Indonesia's most famous artists all over the world. Ambon is recognised by UNESCO as a 'City of Music' and many of the songs we sing are folk songs from there.

The song on the next page is called Nusaniwe, named after a district of Ambon city. Ambon has traditionally used its folk songs as a way to help keep peace and spread unity across the islands.

The Pindito band (right). Overpage: Edi's brother-in-law Toto (right) and Adrian (left) lead the band on guitar.

Nusaniwe

Ho-uu hu-uu ho-ye-ye-ee he-ee
Ho-uu hu-uu ho-ye-ye-ee he-ee

Nusaniwe, Tanjung Alang, Labuhan Raja
Nusaniwe, Tanjung Alang, Labuhan Raja

Pasir putih Tanjung Benteng manise
The white sand of Tanjung Benteng Manise

Kapal-kapal yang berlabuh pun berlayar
The ships that were anchored sailed

Masuk Ambon dan keluar Ambone
Enter Ambon and exit Ambone

Apa tempo kulihat lagi
When will I see you again

Ambon tanah asalku
Ambon is my native land

Jikalau sudah sampai ke tanah Jawa
If you have reached Java

Jangan lupa nona kabaya, oo!
Don't forget Miss Kabaya, oo!

Hu-uu x 2
Boo-hoo x2

Ha-aa-uu
Ha-aa-uu

Ha-aa hu-uu
Ha-aa hoo-uu

Nusaniwe, Tanjung Alang, Labuhan Raja
Nusaniwe, Tanjung Alang, Labuhan Raja

Pasir putih Tanjung Benteng manise
The white sand of Tanjung Benteng Manise

Kapal-kapal yang berlabuh pun berlayar
The ships that were anchored sailed

Masuk Ambon dan keluar Ambone
Enter Ambon and exit Ambone

Apa tempo kulihat lagi
When will I see you again

Ambon tanah asalku
Ambon is my native land

Jikalau sudah sampai ke tanah Jawa
If you have reached Java

Jangan lupa nona kabaya, oo!
Don't forget Miss Kabaya, oo!

Jikalau sudah sampai ke tanah Jawa
If you have reached Java

Jangan lupa nona kabaya, oo!
Don't forget Miss Kabaya, oo!

Jikalau sudah sampai ke tanah Jawa
If you have reached Java

Jangan lupa nona kabaya, ho-ho-oo-oo, sy-ud-ud-ud-ud-ud-ud-u
Don't forget Miss Kabaya, ho-ho-oo-oo, sy-ud-ud-ud-ud-ud-ud-u

Miss kabaya, ye-he-he-he ho-oo-oo
Nona kabaya, ye-he-he-he ho-oo-oo

RECIPES TO TAKE HOME

Pumpkin Cake

Flour	200 g
Sugar	125 g
Butter	150 g
Coconut milk	100 ml
Eggs	2
Pumpkin	400 g
Milk powder	60 g
Bicarbonate of soda	1/2 tsp
Vanilla essence	2 drops

Mix the sugar and egg in a bowl, then add the butter and mix until smooth. Sift the flour then slowly add this and all remaining ingredients, mixing well. Cook for 40 minutes at 170°C.

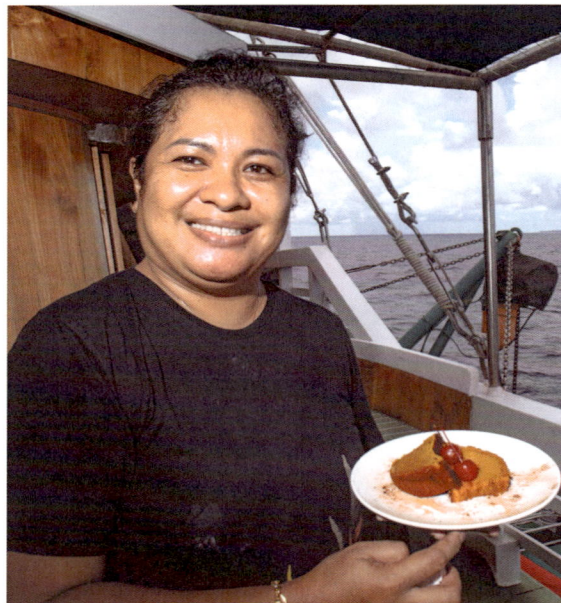

Nasi Goreng

Cooked rice (day-old rice works best)	2 cups
Vegetable oil	2 tbsp
Garlic	2 cloves
Small onion	1 small
Red chillies (optional)	1–2
Mixed vegetables	1/2 cup
Egg	1
Sweet soy sauce (kecap manis)	2 tbsp
Regular soy sauce	1 tbsp

Nasi Goreng (meaning Fried Rice) is an Indonesian staple dish. You can cook it with any other ingredients you have on hand, including fish, chicken and beef. Here is a basic recipe you can adapt to suit your taste!

Nasi Goreng is best prepared using day old or pre-cooled rice as it absorbs flavours and is less sticky. Begin by heating the oil in a pan and stir frying minced garlic, onion (finely chopped) and chopped chillies for a minute or so, until soft. Add the vegetables and stir fry for another 2-3 minutes until tender. Then add the rice. Break up any clumps and stir fry before adding sweet soy sauce and regular soy sauce (but not too much). Stir well until evenly coated then add salt and pepper to taste. Garnish with fried shallots and pop a fried egg on top! You can also mix in fresh green onions, tomato slices and cumumber.

The Captain's dinner is a traditional celebratory feast. On the final night Pindito chooses a guest of honour who gets to cut the top off the rice.

ABOUT THE AUTHOR

Simon's first book 'Wildlife in the Balance' was described by Ian Redmond OBE as 'perhaps the most important book of our time.' His second book 'How to Survive the Next 100 Years: Lessons from Nature' explores the hidden power of nature in all our lives and what we can learn from it.

Simon has worked internationally as an ecologist, expeditioner and conservationist. During a passionate thirty years as researcher, communicator and consultant he has witnessed first-hand, many oblique and candid interactions we have with nature. Simon has led WWF researchers into the heart of oil spills, trekked in the remote jungles of Madagascar, produced Australia's epic National Landscapes film series, and worked for the likes of the RSPB and BirdLife International.

Simon continues to play an active role as adviser to important ecosystem restoration initiatives and regularly joins guests aboard Pindito to explore the coral reefs of Indonesia.

www.simonmustoe.blog

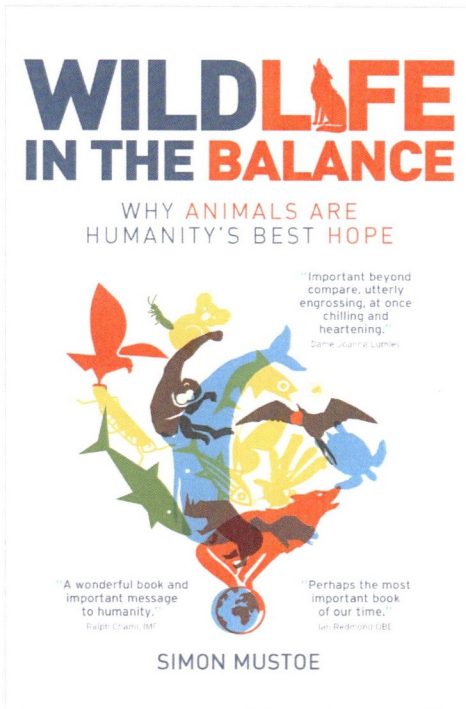

WILDLIFE IN THE BALANCE

WHY ANIMALS ARE HUMANITY'S BEST HOPE

"Important beyond compare, utterly engrossing, at once chilling and heartening."
Dame Joanna Lumley

"A wonderful book and important message to humanity."
Ralph Chami, IMF

"Perhaps the most important book of our time."
Ian Redmond OBE

SIMON MUSTOE

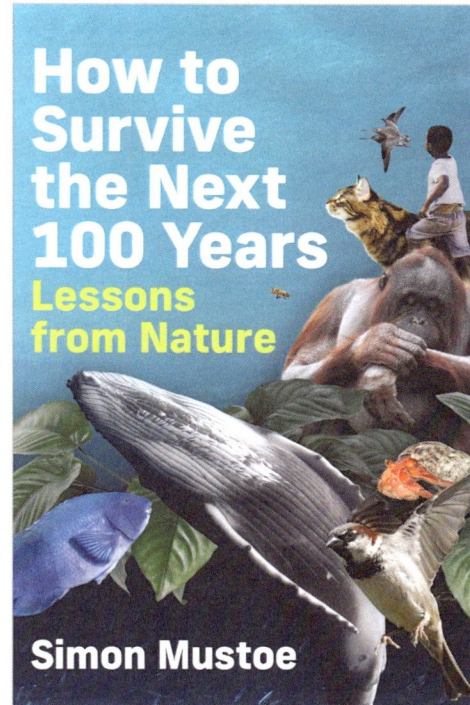

How to Survive the Next 100 Years

Lessons from Nature

Simon Mustoe

Available from all good book stores

Or visit Simon's website or search online.

www.ingramcontent.com/pod-product-compliance
Lightning Source LLC
Chambersburg PA
CBRC0915362=0326
41914CB000213/1637